NATIONAL
GEOGRAPHIC
KiDS

GO WiLD!

Lemurs

Alli Brydon

NATIONAL GEOGRAPHIC
WASHINGTON, D.C.

Bounce ...
climb.
Leap,
slide!

Lemurs like to have a good time.

They hang out in trees or roam the ground
on their very special island home.

Let's explore the world of lemurs!

Home Sweet Home

Lemurs live on the island of Madagascar. They jump and play in lush forests, on stony mountains, and in wet swamps.

Some lemurs live down on the ground.
But most feel at home up in a leafy tree.

Island Life

ARCTIC OCEAN

NORTH AMERICA

EUROPE

ASIA

ATLANTIC OCEAN

AFRICA

PACIFIC OCEAN

PACIFIC OCEAN

SOUTH AMERICA

INDIAN OCEAN

AUSTRALIA

↑ Madagascar

SOUTHERN OCEAN

ANTARCTICA

Madagascar is a large island off the coast of Africa.

Madagascar is the fourth largest island in the world.

INDIAN OCEAN

AFRICA

Madagascar

Mozambique Channel

INDIAN OCEAN

FOSSA

PANTHER CHAMELEON

TOMATO FROG

The land is made up of beaches, deserts, forests, and mountains.

Many of the island's plants and animals are not found anywhere else. Fossas, panther chameleons, and tomato frogs also call the island home.

Big and Small

MADAME BERTHE'S
MOUSE LEMUR

The smallest lemur is the Madame Berthe's mouse lemur.

This tiny lemur is the size of a mouse. It weighs only one ounce (35 g). That's about the same as a slice of bread. Its body is just four inches (10 cm) long, about the length of three paper clips lined up. But its five-inch (13-cm) tail more than doubles its body length!

INDRI

The largest lemur is the indri.

Its body is between two and three feet (0.6 and 0.9 m) long. That's about the length of a baseball bat! It can weigh up to 22 pounds (10 kg), about the same as a car tire.

Do you know any other animals that size?

A Lot of Lemurs!

There are more than 100 species of lemurs.

Aye-Aye
If an aye-aye gets excited or frightened, its long white hairs stick out from its black fur.

Black-and-White Ruffed Lemur
Pollen gets stuck to the ruffs of fur on this lemur, then gets spread around the forest.

Red Ruffed Lemur
This red-colored lemur has the loudest barking voice of all!

Gray Mouse Lemur
The gray mouse lemur mostly munches on beetles.

Indri
The indri clings to trees with large hands and feet.

Crowned Lemur

Both male and female crowned lemurs have "crowns" of fur on their heads.

Mongoose Lemur

This lemur can be active during the day and night, depending on the season.

Blue-Eyed Black Lemur

Not all blue-eyed black lemurs are actually black! Only the males are black; the females are orange-brown.

Red-Bellied Lemur

Male red-bellied lemurs will carry around their babies, just like the females do.

Ring-Tailed Lemur

This lemur searches for fruit and hunts for caterpillars on the ground and in trees.

Check Me Out!

The ring-tailed lemur has black, gray, and white fur, circles around its eyes, and a striped tail.

Two big eyes help it see well.

With its little ears, it hears the calls from its fellow troop members.

A lemur has a great sense of smell. Its nose is on its snout.

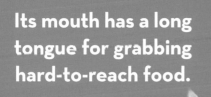

Its mouth has a long tongue for grabbing hard-to-reach food.

Its fur is thick and silky.

Long arms and legs are great for climbing trees and swinging from branches.

Strong, gripping hands and feet each have five fingers or toes.

Its furry tail is longer than its body.

Leaping Lemurs

A lemur's body is made for climbing and jumping. It pushes off a branch with powerful legs and grabs the next branch with long arms.

Most lemurs can jump a distance that is six times their body length.

Look at this lemur leap through the air!

Precious Primates

Lemurs are related to monkeys, apes, tarsiers, galagos, and pottos. What do these animals have in common? They are all primates.

You know what else is a primate? You!

tarsier

monkey

potto

ape

galago

Lemurs have lived on the island of Madagascar for a long time. Over many years, they have become different from their cousins.

Unlike other primates, lemurs have wet noses, a great sense of smell, and eyes that reflect light.

What's for Lunch?

Leaves, fruits, and insects—YUM! Most lemurs eat fruit, leaves, flowers, tree sap, and even tree bark.

Many are omnivores, which means they eat both plants and animals such as insects. And some lemurs are folivores. They eat only leaves.

One of a lemur's favorite foods is tamarind, a juicy, podlike fruit found in trees.

22

When a lemur gets thirsty, it drinks water off leaves, from puddles, or wherever it is wet!

So how does a lemur find a meal? It prowls around and gathers what it can.

Sometimes, there is not enough food. But lemurs have adapted, or changed their behavior, to get by. They eat as much as they can when the trees are full. This helps them get through times when the trees are empty.

Troop Life

What's up, buddy? Lemurs live in groups called troops. Most troops have only four or five lemurs, but some species have troops of up to 20 or 30.

One female is usually the troop's leader. She decides where they will go and guides them to food and shelter.

Squeaky Clean

Lemurs get dirty while climbing around Madagascar. But they don't stay that way for long!

The lemurs in a troop groom themselves and each other. They pick mud, leaves, and insects out of their long fur.

Lemurs have special claws, teeth, and tongues for cleaning, combing, and picking.

This long toenail is called a toilet claw! It can pick through fur.

comb teeth

Lemurs have a group of teeth that they use just like a comb! They even have a special second tongue for cleaning their teeth after grooming.

Awww ... So Cute!

Baby lemurs are called infants. They look just like their mom and dad, but smaller and oh-so-cute!

Infants stick to their moms like glue. It's true! For the first three weeks, lemur infants are carried on their mother's belly. For the next few months, they ride on her back.

Young lemurs in a troop love to play: They chase, nip, and wrestle with each other!

Most lemur mothers give birth to one or two babies at a time.

At birth:
Newborn ring-tailed lemurs are small, furry, and cute.

0–3 weeks:
Babies ride on their mama's belly.

2 weeks:
Ring-tailed lemurs eat solid food and drink their mama's milk.

3–4 weeks:
Ring-tailed lemurs start to climb on their own.

4 months:
Most time is
now spent away
from Mama.

5-6 months:
No more milk! It eats
only gathered food.

1–3 years:
A ring-tailed lemur
lives on its own.
At three years old,
it is all grown up.

Talk to Me

Lemurs snort, howl, scream, and chirp. They use these sounds to "speak" to each other.

This is what scientists think their sounds might mean:

HMM = "Hi, friend!"

32

SHRIEK = "Warning, danger is near!"

PURR = "I'm here, baby."

SCREAM = "Get away!"

33

Most small lemurs are nocturnal, or awake at night. Most large lemurs are diurnal, or awake during the day.

Lemurs also help make things grow! They drop seeds when they eat fruit and when they poop.

Male ring-tailed lemurs can make their tails smell bad and then wave them at their enemies. This is called stink fighting.

Lemurs have wet noses, just like dogs do!

The indri is the largest living lemur, but there used to be a larger species the size of a gorilla!

Black-and-white ruffed lemurs are the only ones that build a nest for their babies. They can have up to six babies at once!

Ring-tailed lemurs can make 22 different sounds.

Lemurs in Trouble

Lemurs have lived on Madagascar for a very long time. At first, there were very few dangers. The fossa is a lemur's main natural predator.

But now lemurs in Madagascar are in trouble because of humans.

People have chopped down trees in the forest, where most lemurs live and eat. Humans have made homes, farms, and roads in the lemurs' habitat.

Now lemurs have little space to live. They also have less food to eat.

I  LEMURS

But people are trying to help lemurs. Some have started groups to protect lemurs and their habitat.

Zoos in Madagascar and all over the world raise and care for lemurs. Many people, including smart kids like you, are learning how to help lemurs!

You Can Help, Too

Do you want to help lemurs? You can adopt one!

This doesn't mean you will take a lemur home as a pet. Instead, you and your family can give money to help lemurs in the wild and at zoos. You can help buy lemurs food, keep them safe, and protect their habitats.

Talk to your local zoo to find out if they have a lemur adoption program.

Lemur Lodge

Lemurs live in different habitats!

Pick out the perfect lemur homes.

forest

ocean

Arctic

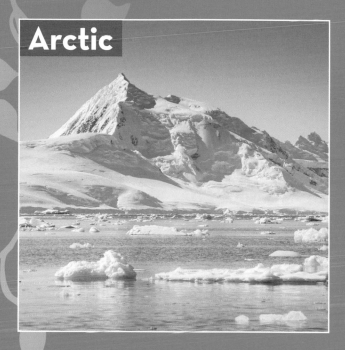

swamp

mountain

city

Lemurs live in forests, swamps, and mountains.

Want to build your child's enthusiasm for lemurs?

There are many ways you can get involved together! Many zoos are home to lemurs. If you can, plan a visit to one to see lemurs in person and learn more about them. And even closer to home, you can go exploring on the internet! Search phrases like "lemur sounds" to hear how they speak, "help lemurs" to find out how to get involved, and "baby lemurs" to see pictures and videos of some aww-inspiring cuties! **Here are some other activities for you and your child to do together.**

 ## Save the Lemurs Poster (Craft)

Want to help save the lemurs? Spread the word! Have your child create a poster to hang at home or at school. Get a large piece of blank paper or poster board and some markers or crayons. Your child can choose their favorite lemur image from this book and draw it at the center of the blank sheet. Then write "SAVE THE LEMURS" at the top. At the bottom, help your child write a few facts about why lemurs are endangered and what we can do to help them.

Play Pretend (Craft and Movement)

Make believe you and your child are lemurs with homemade costumes. For the mask, get a white paper plate, some crayons, construction paper, glue, and some yarn. Help your child cut eye holes in the middle of the plate. Cut two triangles out of construction paper to make the ears and attach them with glue to the top of the paper plate. Have your child draw a nose and mouth, then color in the lemur mask with red, brown, gray, or black crayons. Punch two holes—one on either side of the plate. Pull yarn through each hole and make knots to secure the yarn. Every lemur needs a tail, too! Fasten an old paper towel tube to your child's pants with a safety pin. Now they're ready to slink, jump, and climb. Make a lemur costume for yourself, and you and your child can groom each other!

 ## Lemur Fact Cards (Test Your Knowledge)

Create a deck of lemur fact cards. Ask your child to choose their favorite lemurs from this book and then draw each lemur on the front of an index card. Help your child write one question about lemurs beneath the picture they drew. On the back, write the answer to that question. Do this several times on different index cards. Your child can bring the fact cards to school, to a playdate, or around the house to share some lemur knowledge!

 ## Visit Madagascar (Cultural Connections)

Madagascar is a beautiful, diverse place, home to lemurs and many other creatures and plants. And you can "visit" right from your own home. The BBC television series *Planet Earth*, *Planet Earth II*, and *Our Planet* all feature Madagascar in several episodes. And of course, the Nat Geo Wild TV channel is perfect for exploring the island and meeting lemurs.

GLOSSARY

adapt: to adjust to changing conditions or environment

diurnal: awake during the day

endangered: when a whole species is in danger of dying out, or becoming extinct

groom: to clean, brush, and tend to oneself or others

habitat: an animal's natural home

nocturnal: awake during the night

omnivores: animals that eat both plants and animals

predators: animals that hunt and eat other animals for food

primates: an order of animals that includes lemurs, monkeys, apes, and humans

species: a group of animals that are closely related and have many of the same characteristics

For Alex, who loves lemurs —A.B.

Cover, G & M Therin Weise/Getty Images; Back cover, Eric Isselee/Shutterstock; 1, Klein & Hubert/naturepl; 5, Jak Wonderly/NGS; 6 (LE), Ellen B. Goff/Danita Delimont/Danita Delimont; 6 (RT), Martin Harvey/Getty Images; 7 (UP LE), Jouan & Rius/naturepl; 7 (UP RT), Otto Plantema/Minden Pictures; 7 (LO), David Pattyn/naturepl; 8, NG Maps; 9 (UP), Lorraine Bennery/naturepl; 9 (LO LE), George Grall/Alamy Stock Photo; 9 (LO RT), Thomas Marent/Minden Pictures; 10, Houdin and Palanque/naturepl; 11, Zoonar GmbH/Alamy Stock Photo; 12 (LE), Chien Lee/Minden Pictures; 12 (RT), Konrad Wothe/Minden Pictures; 13 (UP), Christian Hutter/Alamy Stock Photo; 13 (LE), Tony Camacho/Science Source; 13 (RT), Andy Rouse/naturepl; 14 (LE), Nick Garbutt/naturepl; 14 (UP RT), Suzi Eszterhas/Minden Pictures; 14 (LO RT), Huetter, C./Imagebroker/Alamy Stock Photo; 15 (UP), Bernard Castelein/naturepl; 15 (LO), Rosanne Tackaberry/Alamy Stock Photo; 16-17 (both), Eric Isselee/Shutterstock; 19, gerard lacz/Alamy Stock Photo; 20 (LE), Thomas Marent/Minden Pictures; 20 (RT), Anup Shah/Minden Pictures; 21 (UP LE), Daniel Heuclin/naturepl; 21 (UP RT), Thomas Marent/Minden Pictures; 21 (CTR), Roland Seitre/Minden Pictures; 22 (LE), Valeriy Tretyakov/iStockphoto/Getty Images; 22 (RT), Anup Shah/Getty Images; 23 (LE), Vince Burton/Alamy Stock Photo; 23 (RT), Alison Jones/Alamy Stock Photo; 25, Cyril Ruoso/Minden Pictures; 26, Zoo-Life/Alamy Stock Photo; 26 (inset), Sara Rowe Clark/Duke Lemur Center; 27, Appfind/iStockphoto/Getty Images; 29, Cyril Ruoso/Minden Pictures; 30 (At birth), Suzi Eszterhas/naturepl; 30 (0-3 weeks), Suzi Eszterhas/naturepl; 30 (2 weeks), iculizard/iStockphoto/Getty Images; 30 (3-4 weeks), PA Images/Alamy Stock Photo; 31 (4 months), Courtesy Rod Kuba; 31 (5-6 months), Suzi Eszterhas/naturepl; 31 (1-3 years), Mike Powles/Science Source; 32, Arterra Picture Library/Alamy Stock Photo; 33 (UP LE), Martin Harvey/Getty Images; 33 (RT), Suzi Eszterhas/Minden Pictures; 33 (LO), RMMPPhotography/Shutterstock; 34-35, Nick Garbutt/naturepl; 36, J-L Klein & M-L Hubert/naturepl; 37, mihtiander/iStockphoto/Getty Images; 38 (LE), The Asahi Shimbun/Getty Images; 38 (UP RT), AP Photo/Jerome Delay; 38 (LO RT), AP Photo/Joana Coutinho; 39 (UP LE), Rebecca Krizak/picture alliance/Getty Images; 39 (CTR LE), Chairat Rattana/iStockphoto/Getty Images; 39 (LO LE), Filippo Monteforte/AFP/Getty Images; 39 (RT), Luis Robayo/AFP/Getty Images; 41, Godong/Alamy Stock Photo; 42 (LE), Otto Plantema/Minden Pictures; 42 (RT), Greens and Blues/Shutterstock; 43 (UP LE), Lua Carlos Martins/Shutterstock; 43 (UP RT), Edwin Giesbers/naturepl; 43 (LO LE), Daisy Gilardini/Danita Delimont; 43 (LO RT), Roschetzky Photography/Shutterstock

Published by National Geographic Partners, LLC, Washington, DC 20036.

Designed by Kathryn Robbins

Hardcover ISBN: 978-1-4263-7254-4
Reinforced library binding ISBN: 978-1-4263-7255-1

The author and publisher wish to acknowledge the expert review of this book by Sara Clark of the Duke Lemur Center and the National Geographic book team: Angela Modany, associate editor; Shelby Lees, senior editor; Sarah J. Mock and Liz Seramur, photo editors; Kathryn Robbins, senior designer; Mike McNey, senior cartographer; Alix Inchausti, production editor; and Anne LeongSon and Gus Tello, design production assistants.

Printed in China
21/PPS/1